The Little
of Healthy Eating

by Amicia Boden
Illustrations by Marion Lindsay

LITTLE BOOKS WITH **BIG** IDEAS

Featherstone Education
An imprint of Bloomsbury Publishing Plc

50 Bedford Square
London
WC1B 3DP
UK

1385 Broadway
New York
NY 10018
USA

www.bloomsbury.com

Text © Amicia Boden, 2016
Illustrations © Marion Lindsay, 2016
Cover photographs ©Shutterstock, 2016

British Library Cataloguing-in-Publication Data
A catalogue record for this book is available from the British Library.

ISBN:
PB 978-1-4729-2253-3
ePDF 978-1-4729-2254-0

Library of Congress Cataloging-in-Publication Data
A catalog record for this book is available from the Library of Congress.

1 3 5 7 9 10 8 6 4 2

Printed and bound in India by Replika Pvt. Ltd

This book is produced using paper that is made from wood grown in managed, sustainable forests. It is natural, renewable and recyclable. The logging and manufacturing processes conform to the environmental regulations of the country of origin.

**To view more of our titles please visit
www.bloomsbury.com**

Contents

Introduction

The Early Years Foundation Stage (EYFS) is a crucial time for setting up healthy eating habits that will continue throughout childhood and beyond. This book offers a varied selection of fun, easy, healthy eating activities to suit different ages, stages and skills. The activities can be used to introduce the children in your setting to healthy eating concepts and, importantly, will also consolidate this learning through exposure to handling, preparing, cooking and tasting a wide variety of foods. Exposure to variety is key here in enabling children to discover and enjoy many different foods for a healthy, balanced diet. The activities also offer valuable learning experiences across the EYFS that link with the Early Learning Goals (ELGs) and contribute towards a healthy eating environment within your setting.

Links with the Early Learning Goals

Integrating healthy eating into your setting supports the EYFS welfare requirement for 'healthy, balanced and nutritious' food and drink and ties in to the ELGs in the following ways.

Communication and language

▶ Language development through learning the names of foods, cooking methods, colours, shapes, textures, temperatures and tastes.

▶ Articulating and expressing individual food sensory experiences; describing taste, texture, smell, temperature, size and appearance of food; answering 'how' or 'why' questions about an experience.

▶ Speaking and listening in different situations.

▶ Conversation and social skills through sitting together to enjoy a meal or snack.

▶ Following instructions involving several ideas or actions, e.g. through recipes.

▶ Opportunities to use past, present and future tenses.

Physical development

▶ Opportunities to be active and interactive.

▶ Development of fine and gross motor skills when preparing food and following physical actions; cooking activities also support the development of control, co-ordination and small movements.

▶ Supporting understanding of healthy choices in relation to food.

▶ Handling cooking equipment and a range of utensils.

▶ Health and self-care in relation to the importance of good health, healthy diet, ways to keep healthy, and basic hygiene.

Personal, social and emotional development

▶ Opportunities to taste different foods and become aware of individual likes and dislikes, and to respect those of others; perhaps even overcome some food dislikes.

▶ Working as part of a group, playing co-operatively and taking turns.

▶ Develop confidence with cooking abilities.

Literacy

▶ Opportunities to look at the many books that involve food, and to explore other reading materials such as food magazines, food packaging, food labels, recipes, fruit and vegetable seed catalogues, shopping lists, signs and posters.

Mathematics

▶ Supporting numeracy skills through counting out ingredients and using spoons or other measures, whilst following recipes; using addition and subtraction when weighing and measuring ingredients.

▶ Supporting organisational skills, reasoning and mathematical language through sorting objects into groups by type/size/volume; matching and pairing objects; describing shapes, spaces and measures.

▶ Developing language to describe size, weight, capacity, position, time and money.

Understanding the world

▶ Opportunities to learn about where food comes from.

▶ Developing knowledge of the community, physical world, environment, special occasions, seasons and cultures across the world through the exploration of food.

▶ Observing animals and plants in relation to the food that we eat.

▶ Developing awareness that other children may have different food likes or dislikes.

▶ Becoming sensitive to similarities and differences surrounding people, families, communities, cultures and traditions.

Expressive arts and design

▶ Opportunities to look at colours, shapes, and sensory qualities of foods, contributing to confidence in handling new foods.

▶ Incorporating songs, rhymes, movement and role-play when learning about healthy eating.

▶ Opportunities to design their own versions of recipes to represent their own ideas.

Healthy eating in the early years

Children who eat a healthy, balanced diet containing a wide variety of foods will generally get enough energy and nutrients for healthy growth and development. However, we do know that the diets of young children in the UK are often too low in vitamins A, C and D and the minerals iron and zinc. Their diets may also be too high in sugar and salt. Another major concern is the significant number of children that are overweight or obese when they enter reception year. The Department of Health recommends that all children aged from 6 months to 5 years be given vitamin drops containing vitamins A, C and D. The communication of consistent messages about healthy eating in the Early Years will have a positive impact upon lifelong healthy eating habits.

The activities in the first half of this book can be used to introduce children to the key concepts of healthy eating. Opportunities include handling different fruits and vegetables and working on language to express taste and texture. Exposure to new fruits and vegetables during fun activities, without pressure to eat, will mean that the children are more likely to eat those fruits and vegetables on another day. The second half of this book consists of cooking activities that can be integrated into cross-curricular topics. These healthy recipes have a particular focus on fruits, vegetables, dairy, fish and desserts that do not require added sugar.

The Eatwell Plate is a graphic that represents the healthy eating advice issued by the government. Information on reproducing the Eatwell Plate graphic and its use in health promotion material can be found on the www.gov.uk website. The Eatwell Plate shows the overall balance of foods from each food group that we should aim for in our diet. It is suitable for most people, with the exception of children under 2 years old, who require a higher proportion of fat in their diet. Between the ages of 2 and 5 years, children may gradually move towards a diet with the balance represented in the Eatwell Plate. The key messages and food groups are:

▶ Eat plenty of fruits and vegetables, aiming for 5 A Day. This includes fresh, canned (no added salt, sugar or syrup) or frozen. Even simply tasting 5 fruits and vegetables each day is a positive step. A total early years portion is 40g. A dried fruit portion represents 20g, and should be limited to mealtimes only as dried fruit can cause tooth decay. For the same reason, if fruit juice is offered it should also be limited to mealtimes and should be diluted (half juice, half water).

▶ Eat plenty of bread, rice, potatoes, pasta and other starchy food. Some of these may be wholegrain.

▶ Eat some milk and dairy foods. In the early years, aim for 3 servings per day from this group. From 2 years old, children may be offered semi-skimmed milk. Full fat cheese, yoghurt and fromage frais may be helpful for children with small appetites. However, from 2 years onwards, reduced fat varieties may be offered if becoming overweight is a concern. Choose lower sugar varieties of yoghurt or select plain ones and add fruit.

▶ Eat some meat, fish, eggs, beans and other non-dairy sources of protein. Opt for lean meats. Eggs should be well cooked. Generally aim to include more fish each week, one of which should be oily. Nuts are included in this group. However, children under 5 should not be offered whole nuts due to the risk of choking. Fine chopped, ground and flaked nuts or nut butters may be suitable but do check up-to-date individual allergy records.

▶ A small amount of food and drink high in saturated fat or added sugar may be included as part of a healthy diet. However, these are best restricted to occasional mealtimes and not everyday. The aim is to reduce intake of foods high in saturated fat, added sugar and salt. Instead, add flavour with fruits and vegetables, lemon, garlic, herbs and spices.

Health, safety and dietary requirements

▶ All staff who prepare and handle food in an Early Years setting should have up-to-date food hygiene training and follow the requirements of the Food Safety Act when delivering the activities in this book.

▶ Support children in adopting good hygiene practices before food activities, such as tying back long hair, removing jewellery, rolling up long sleeves, washing and drying hands, and putting on a kitchen apron.

▶ Follow health and safety principles by cleaning and clearing surfaces of any hazards, avoid leaving the children once the activity has begun, and appropriately manage equipment using safe techniques.

▶ Check all child records for notification of allergies or intolerances prior to every cooking activity. Ensure that these records are kept up-to-date. Carefully read food packaging and labels prior to each activity.

▶ For the recipes in this book, if dairy-free alternatives are required do source calcium-fortified varieties. Where butter is used, this can be substituted with dairy-free spread. Where cheese is used, this may be substituted with dairy-free cheese alternatives available in most supermarkets. Do test the recipe in advance, however, as the melting quality and taste will vary.

▶ An egg replacement product can be used as an alternative in baked recipes if egg-free is required. Follow the manufacturer's guidance and test the recipe in advance.

▶ If using gluten-free or wheat-free flour, seek the manufacturer's guidance on how to adapt the recipe and test it in advance.

▶ If there are children in your setting who follow a special diet (due to allergy or intolerance, medical need, vegetarian, vegan, or any cultural, ethnic or religious diets), when using food models or food images during healthy eating education sessions do include examples that would be suitable for their special diet. This will ensure that they are fully included and will enable them to acquire healthy eating knowledge that is appropriate to their individual needs.

Getting started

▶ The activities are for groups of 4-6 children unless specified otherwise.

▶ The cooking activities involve table-based preparation, followed by eating, baking or chilling the food or drink, without multiple stages. They should therefore be practical for most settings. Instead of using a hob, the recipes requiring heat have been adapted for use in an oven so that both adults and children may move onto other activities during the cooking time.

▶ The recipes have been tested using a conventional fan-assisted oven and could be adapted for table top mini ovens, halogen ovens or microwave ovens (using the oven setting), according to the equipment available in your setting. Consult your product manual for any necessary adjustments in temperature or cooking times. Test-run recipes in the oven in your setting in advance.

▶ The cooking activities can be adapted according to ages and stages. For example, with younger children you could pre-weigh most of the ingredients and do the chopping before starting the activity. With one-to-one time or with a group of older children, you could involve them more in the stages of weighing out ingredients and support them in washing, chopping and grating vegetables using suitable equipment and safe techniques.

▶ Balance scales can be a great way to involve young children in weighing out ingredients by adding more or taking away until the target weight is reached. Rotary graters that fix securely to the table can be a fun and physical activity for young children. Crinkle cutters may be an ergonomic introduction to chopping and slicing soft fruits and vegetables. Child-size cooking equipment, mixing bowls with handles, and non-slip mats can make the activities more accessible. Clean nursery scissors, reserved for kitchen use only, can enable young children to prepare certain vegetables and herbs.

Conversion tables

Weight

| Imperial | | Metric | |
Ounces (oz)	Pounds (lb)	Grams (g)	Kilos (kg)
1		28	
2		56	
3 1/2		100	
4	1/4	112	
5		140	
6		168	
8	1/2	225	
9		250	1/4
12	3/4	340	
16	1	450	
18		500	1/2
20	1 1/4	560	
24	1 1/2	675	
27		750	3/4
28	1 3/4	780	
32	2	900	
36	2 1/4	1000	1
40	2 1/2	1100	
48	3	1350	
54		1500	1 1/2

Temperature

Celsius (°C)	Fahrenheit (°F)
150	300
160	325
180	350
190	375
200	400
220	425
230	450

Activities

The Eatwell Plate

Focus
Getting to know the Eatwell Plate and its five food groups. Learning that we need a variety of foods to be healthy.

Skills
Sorting and organising foods into different food groups.

What you need:

▶ A large Eatwell Plate floor/table mat or poster.

▶ A tray displaying a selection of foods (real or model) or food pictures from each of the five food groups, e.g. bread roll, potato, packet of pasta, banana, mushroom, broccoli head, can of beans, can of tuna, block of cheese, yoghurt, crisp packet, chocolate wrapper.

What you do:

1. Look at the Eatwell Plate together and explain that it shows us that we need a variety of different foods to be healthy.

2. Ask the children to look and tell you what they notice. For example, a plate, a knife and fork, particular foods, colours, groups.

3. Count the different food groups together. Ask the children which two groups are the largest. Which group is the smallest? Which two groups are medium sized? What types of foods can they spot in these groups? Use this to talk about how, in order to stay healthy, we need lots of foods from the fruits and vegetables and starchy foods groups, we need some foods from the dairy and protein food groups, and a little from the high fat and high sugar food group is OK so long as it's not every day.

4. Ask the children to take turns sorting food items from the tray and placing them on the Eatwell Plate in the food group that they belong to.

And another idea:

▶ Use the Eatwell Plate to explore and sort foods from around the world.

▶ Go outside and chalk up a large blank Eatwell Plate on the ground, or use five large hoops to represent each of the different food groups. Ask each child to hold a food item, model or picture and to hop, skip or jump to stand in the correct food group.

▶ Ask the children to cut and stick (or draw) pictures of their favourite foods onto A4 Eatwell Plate posters. These could be laminated and taken home as placemats.

Just right!

Focus
Different sized people need different sized portions of food.

Skills
Sorting and pairing objects by size.

What you need:

▶ Three toy bears: large, medium and small

▶ Three bowls: large, medium and small

▶ A large tub filled with porridge oats (uncooked)

▶ A picture book of 'Goldilocks and the Three Bears'

What you do:

1. Read 'Goldilocks and the Three Bears' with the children. Ask the children to guess who each bowl/chair/bed belongs to.

2. Show the children the three toy bears. Ask the children which bear is the biggest, which is the smallest, and which is medium-sized. Which bear do they think could be daddy bear? Which could be baby bear?

3. Set the scene for a game in which the children will serve the three bears their porridge. Take the opportunity to talk about how important breakfast is to give our bodies energy for the day. We are all different sizes, so we all need a different-sized breakfast that is just right for us.

4. Ask the children to take turns putting porridge oats into the three bowls: two handfuls into the first bowl, four handfuls into the second bowl, and six handfuls into the third bowl. Encourage the children to join in counting the handfuls out loud.

5. Ask the children to sort the bowls according to how many porridge oats they contain. Which bowl contains the most? Which contains the least? Which bowl is in between?

6. Encourage the children to work together to choose which bowl of porridge oats would be just right for daddy, for mummy, and for baby bear. Ask them to place the bears next to their bowls.

7. Reinforce the concept of different sized people needing different sized portions of food to fuel their bodies. Ask the children clench one of their fists, and tell them that this can be used as a rough starting point to measure how big our own food portion sizes should be. We should also listen to our tummies to see if we need more to feel satisfied (not stuffed!).

And another idea:

▶ Consolidate the activity by making porridge with the children. Ask each child to serve a portion into their own bowl, using their clenched fist as a rough size guide. Offer a selection of fruit toppings for them to pick and mix from.

▶ Fill a sand table or tray with porridge oats, spoons, saucepans and bowls for an imaginative play session.

My mealtimes

Focus

Become familiar with the concept of having a regular mealtime routine. This activity works best when carried out in very small groups, in order to offer the children plenty of support, depending on how old they are and their stage of development.

Skills

Cutting and sticking; recognising that a clock face represents a time of day.

What you need:

▶ 3 sheets of A4 paper per child, folded in half and stapled to create portrait an A5 booklet

▶ A photograph of each child, or self-portrait they have painted

▶ 5 blank clock face print-outs, without clock hands or numerals (each small enough to fit an A5 portrait sheet)

▶ A selection of food pictures (from food magazines or printed) showing examples of breakfast, lunch, dinner, snacks and drinks relevant to the children in your setting

▶ Child-safe scissors and glue sticks

What you do:

1. Prepare the booklets for the activity in advance by printing the title 'My Mealtimes' on the front, sticking a photograph of the child (or his/her self-portrait) on the front, and leaving a space for their name to be written (with support if required). The booklet will have five double-page spreads, and each one should be labelled: breakfast, morning snack, midday meal, afternoon snack, and evening meal (adapt mealtime names according to common use in your local setting). Stick a clock face onto the left hand page of each double-page spread and draw on the clock hands and the relevant numerals to show a time for each corresponding meal or snack, e.g. 7:30am, 10:00am, 12:00pm, 2:30pm, 5:00pm.

2. Start the activity by talking with the children about how our bodies need regular meals and drinks in order to be healthy and have energy for the day. Get the children to talk through their own mealtime routine. Prompt them by asking: "Who had breakfast today?", "What did you eat?", "Did you have a drink?", "What did we have at morning snack today?", and so on.

3. Give the children their personalised 'My Mealtimes' booklet. Support them in writing their names on the front covers. Show them the pages inside and explain that they are going to cut and stick pictures of foods and drinks onto each right-hand page to show their mealtime routine.

4. Work through each of the mealtimes, taking the opportunity to look at the clock faces and ask questions such as "What number is the big hand pointing to?" Talk about the time of day, the meal or snack time, what the children like to eat at this time, and ask them to choose food pictures and a drink picture to stick onto the right hand side of the double-page spread. Continue until the 'My Mealtimes' booklet is completed.

And another idea:

▶ Adapt the difficulty level of the activity as you see fit, e.g. consider simplifying it to a colouring activity for younger children, or encourage older children to complete the clock faces themselves for a more advanced focus on time.

▶ Play a game using an analogue clock teaching aid and a selection of plastic food, and cups labelled with the names of various drinks. Change the time on the clock and call out the mealtime. The children should jump up and choose a relevant food or drink. Act out the mealtime together.

5-a-day

Focus

Introduce the concept of eating five portions of fruit and vegetables every day.

Skills

Counting up to 5; literacy and language surrounding colours and names of fruits and vegetables.

What you need:

▶ A large Eatwell Plate poster

▶ Role-play area set up as a greengrocer's, with a variety of fruits and vegetables on display, aprons, weighing scales, shopping baskets, cash register and play money, etc.

▶ Prepared laminated shopping lists, each showing five pictures of different fruits and vegetables (that are available in the Greengrocer's role-play area), with each item numbered 1 to 5.

What you do:

1. Show the children the poster of the Eatwell Plate. Ask the children to point to the fruit and vegetable food group. Ask whether it is one of the largest groups or one of the smallest groups. Explain that it is one of the largest groups because we need to eat lots of different fruits and vegetables each day to give our bodies vitamins and fibre to help us stay healthy. Ask the children to hold up one of their hands and count the five fingers. Explain that we need to eat five portions of fruit and vegetables each day, which is known as 5-a-day!

2. A portion of fruit or vegetables for this age group is 40g, but it is more practical to encourage the children to think of one portion as a handful (the size of one of their clenched fists).

3. Ask the children to each name their favourite fruit or vegetable. What colour is it? What does it taste like? What meal or snack time do they eat it at?

4. Show the children the 'greengrocer's' role-play area. Encourage the children to name the fruits and vegetables that they recognise. Name any unfamiliar ones, and encourage them to touch, smell, explore and verbalise their sensory experience for any unfamiliar fruits and vegetables.

5. Divide the children into the roles of shoppers and greengrocers. Ask the shoppers to buy the five fruits and vegetables on their shopping list. Come together at the end of the game to explore what they have in their shopping baskets.

And another idea:

▶ Extend this activity by preparing some of the fruits and vegetables for a tasting opportunity. Show the children how to gauge a portion size by using their handful as a guide.

▶ For some hands-on experience, go on a real shopping trip to a greengrocer's, a fruit and vegetable market, or a 'pick your own' farm.

▶ Adapt the shopping game to fit specific themes, such as fruits and vegetables from a certain season or a particular part of the world.

Funny faces

Focus

A familiarisation activity to develop confidence with handling unfamiliar vegetables. The focus is on fun and exploration in order to increase the appeal of different vegetables.

Skills

Engaging with food through expressive art and design; identifying colours and shapes; literacy and language surrounding colours and names of vegetables.

What you need:

▶ Paper plates

▶ A selection of vegetables, both in their natural state and prepared in different forms. For example:

▷ Broad beans in pods and shelled

▷ Sweetcorn on the cob, and loose drained kernels from a can (with no added salt or sugar)

▷ Tomatoes on the vine, and halved cherry tomatoes

▷ Sugar snap peas and shelled peas

▷ Whole red, yellow and orange bell peppers, and also sliced and/or diced

▷ Whole carrots with green tops, and carrots sliced into sticks and/or rounds

▷ Whole sweet potato, and roasted wedges

▷ Whole beetroot with tops, and beetroot cut into chunks once cooked (you can buy precooked vacuum-packed beetroot without vinegar)

▷ Whole broccoli, and broccoli cut into florets

▷ If you have access to a vegetable spiral slicer it can be used with carrots or courgettes to make fantastic noodle-like 'hair'; also provide the vegetables whole.

What you do:

1. Ask the children to tell you which vegetables they recognise. Name any unfamiliar vegetables with the children. Pass around each of the 'natural state' vegetables and encourage language to describe the size, texture, weight and smell.

2. Give each child a paper plate. Draw their attention to the prepared vegetables. What shapes can you see? Ask the children to use the prepared vegetable pieces to create colourful and funny vegetable faces on their paper plates. Younger ones may need some prompting. What could you use for eyes? What else do we have on our faces? Where does the nose go?

3. Encourage the children to verbalise how the different prepared vegetables feel. What do they smell like? Do they snap or bend? Do encourage prodding, squashing, smelling, licking or tasting, as this all helps to develop the confidence to try eating different vegetables.

4. Photograph the children's finished funny vegetable faces and print the images for them as a keepsake to take home. Arrange their plates on a display table, alongside the whole vegetables in their natural state.

And another idea:

▶ This activity can be easily adapted to fruit exploration, or different themes such as 'colours', 'world foods' or 'seasons'.

▶ Try keeping fruit and vegetable exploration logbooks to document each child's experience in touching, smelling, licking and tasting fruits and vegetables.

▶ Consolidate with literacy materials. For example, fruit and vegetable A to Z picture books (such as 'Eating the Alphabet' by Lois Ehlert), fruit and vegetable seed catalogues or allotment magazines with lots of colour images.

Rainbow cups

Focus

A fun familiarisation activity to develop confidence with handling unfamiliar fruits. The focus is on exploration, in order to increase the appeal of different types of fruit.

Skills

Engaging with food through expressive art and design; identifying the colours of the rainbow and colour matching; literacy and language surrounding colours and names of fruits; physical development with fine motor skills in handling small objects.

What you need:

▶ Poster showing a rainbow (laminated if possible)

▶ Disposable clear plastic drinking cups

▶ One fruit to represent each colour of the rainbow: both in its whole form and also prepared into bite sized pieces, in bowls with dessert spoons. Choices could include:

▷ Red: cherries, red apples, strawberries, raspberries, watermelon, pomegranate, red grapes

▷ Orange: satsumas, oranges, apricots, tangerines, peaches, nectarines, cantaloupe melon, mango

21

- ▷ Yellow: pineapple, galia melon, bananas, star fruit, yellow grapefruit, lemons, golden raspberries
- ▷ Green: kiwi fruit, green apples, green grapes, limes, gooseberries, pears, raw fresh figs, greengages, honeydew melon
- ▷ Blue/purple: blueberries, blackberries, blackcurrants, plums, black grapes

What you do:

1. Look at the rainbow poster with the children. Ask them to name the colours one by one.

2. Take one of the whole fruits and pass it around. Encourage the children to explore the feel and smell of each fruit. Ask questions such as: 'Does anyone know what this fruit is called?' 'Has anyone tasted it before?' 'What colour is it?' 'What does it smell like?'

3. Ask the children to place each fruit on the rainbow poster, matching up the fruit with the correct colour on the rainbow.

4. Look at the fruit rainbow you have created as a class. Explain that different colour fruits provide us with different nutrients to help keep our bodies healthy. That is why we try to eat a rainbow of fruits and vegetables every day.

5. Give each child a plastic cup. Ask them to scoop layers of the prepared fruit into their cups, colour by colour, to make a rainbow-striped fruit cup. Do praise any incidental touching, prodding, squashing, smelling, licking or tasting: this all helps to develop the confidence to taste different fruits.

6. Look at the colours showing through the side of the cup. Ask the children to describe what it looks like.

7. Enjoy the rainbow cups at a meal or snack time.

And another idea:

- ▶ For a focus on fine motor skills and handgrip strength, try offering clean tongs for use when transferring the fruit pieces into the cups.

- ▶ Use wooden skewers or cake-pop sticks to make rainbow fruit kebabs.

- ▶ Try keeping fruit and vegetable exploration logbooks in order to document each child's experience of touching, smelling, licking, and tasting fruits and vegetables.

- ▶ Consolidate with literacy materials (such as 'Handa's Surprise' by Eileen Browne), fruit and vegetable A to Z picture books (such as 'Eating the Alphabet' by Lois Ehlert), fruit and vegetable seed catalogues or allotment magazines with lots of colour images.

Let's go fishing!

Focus

Thinking about the benefits of including fish in our diet, and familiarisation with the concept of eating more fish in our snacks and meals.

Skills

Literacy and language surrounding appearance and names of fish and fish dishes; physical development using fine motor skills.

What you need:

▶ Eatwell Plate poster

▶ Fishpond (you could use a small empty paddling pool, a large sheet of blue paper, or a large shatterproof play mirror)

▶ Magnetic fishing rods. If you don't have any, make some using wooden rods, sticks or dowels. Tie a length of string to one end and securely attach a small magnet to the other end of the string.

▶ Fish: cut out images of fish, laminate, and attach a split pin close to the mouth so that they can be 'caught' with the magnetic fishing rods. To optimise learning about these foods, try to source images of real fish. Include a few images for fun. For example:

▷ Salmon

▷ Mackerel

▷ Tinned tuna

▷ Cod

▷ Haddock

▷ Prawns

▷ Cod fish fingers

▷ Salmon fish cakes

▷ Tuna sandwich

▷ Fish pie

▷ Prawn stir fry

▷ Mackerel paté on toast

What you do:

1. Look at the Eatwell Plate poster. Can anyone see which food group has some fish in it? Explain that the fish are in the protein food group, and that eating more fish helps us to grow. Oily fish (such as salmon and mackerel) are good for our hearts and brains.

2. Encourage the children to talk about any fish or fish dish that they like to eat.

3. Play the 'Let's go fishing' game. The children take it in turns to catch something from the fishpond using a magnetic fishing rod. Whilst fishing, encourage everyone to chant: '1, 2, 3, let's catch a fish for tea! 1, 2, 3, it's going to taste YUMMY!'

4. Ask the children if they can name which fish has been caught, and discuss it as a group. Is it an oily fish, such as salmon or mackerel? Is it a white fish, such as cod or haddock? Is it seafood, such as prawns? Has anyone tasted it before?

5. When each child has had a go, come together to all sing the song 'Once I caught a fish alive'.

And another idea:

▶ Consolidate by making a quick and simple fish dish together, such as a tuna sandwich or mackerel paté on toast.

▶ Try the fish dish cooking activities provided in this book (crispy salmon balls, and vegetable and prawn Chinese rolls).

Build your bones

Focus

Introduce the relationship between dairy foods and bone health.

Skills

Literacy and language surrounding dairy foods; numeracy; following physical activity instructions; turn-taking.

What you need:

▶ Open space with room to move – ideally outdoors in the sunshine!

▶ Eatwell Plate poster

▶ Display table

▶ Large numeral 3 cut out in bright card together with a fun skeleton poster – both placed on the display table

▶ Selection of dairy foods (enough for the children to each choose 3 foods). For example: small cartons of milk (100-150ml), 125g pots of yoghurt, wrapped portions of cheese (enough for a sandwich filling), small pots of custard or rice pudding, small pots of cream cheese, examples of calcium-enriched dairy alternatives

▶ A physical activity instruction label attached to each of the dairy foods. For example: 3 hops, 3 star jumps, 3 toe touches, 3 big jumps, 3 feet stamps, 3 arm flaps

What you do:

1. Look at the milk and dairy foods section on the Eatwell Plate. Ask the children to name the foods that they can spot in this section. Ask about their favourites and talk about calcium-enriched dairy alternatives that people might eat if they do not eat dairy. This is a good opportunity to talk about how dairy foods are made from cow's milk.

2. What size is the dairy section on the Eatwell Plate? It shows us that we need to eat some dairy foods each day. This age group need three servings of dairy food each day to give them protein to help their bodies grow and calcium for growing strong healthy bones and teeth.

3. Introduce the idea that for strong healthy bones we need calcium from foods, vitamin D from sunlight on our skin and vitamin supplements, and we need to move our bodies with plenty of physical activity.

4. Have a look at the selection of dairy foods and calcium-enriched alternatives on the display table.

5. Play the 'Build your bones' game, where the children take turns to choose a dairy food from the table. Then everyone follows the attached physical activity instruction label, such as 'do 3 hops'. Continue until all of the children have chosen three servings of dairy foods each.

6. Finish by arranging all of the dairy foods back onto the display table in the shape of the numeral '3', using the card cut-out as a guide. Reinforce the key messages of eating three servings of dairy foods each day, and getting enough sunshine and vitamin D supplements together with plenty of physical activity to build your bones.

And another idea:

▶ Have a tasting session and talk about the children's favourite dairy foods (or calcium enriched alternatives).

▶ Try one of the recipes in this book that includes dairy in the ingredients.

▶ Make skeleton pictures to add to the 'Build your bones' display table by sticking cut-out skull faces onto sheets of black paper and sticking on white cotton buds for the bones.

Wake up, taste buds!

Focus

Working on language to express experiences of taste. The 'Hugh's hair salad' recipe in this book can be combined with this activity to consolidate the learning.

Skills

Language skills to label and describe sensory experiences of taste.

What you need:

▶ 5 small egg cups per child, containing examples of different tastes:

  ▷ Sweet: 1 teaspoon of honey

  ▷ Sour: 1 teaspoon of lemon juice

  ▷ Bitter: small pinch of lemon zest

  ▷ Salty and Umami: 1/2 teaspoon of soy sauce

  ▷ Spicy: 1/4 teaspoon of minced ginger

▶ Bread sticks

▶ Jug of water and drinking cups

▶ Small hand mirrors

What you do:

1. Ask the children to think about which part of their bodies they taste things with.

2. Ask them to have a close look at their own tongue in the hand mirrors. Who can see their tiny taste buds? Talk about how when we eat food, the taste buds on our tongues help us to notice different tastes.

3. Ask the children to look at their five egg cups, and explain that they each contain different tastes. One is sweet, one is sour, one is bitter, one is salty and umami (a meaty/savoury taste), and one is spicy.

4. Time to explore the different tastes and wake up your taste buds! Start with the 'sweet' egg cup. Can anyone guess what is in the egg cup? Encourage the children to smell the contents. Without any pressure, invite them to use a breadstick to taste a tiny bit. Children that are reluctant to taste can be encouraged to smell or touch and maybe lick their fingers. Have cups of water on hand to sip between tasting. Ask: 'What does it taste like?' Try to reframe words such as 'yum' or 'yuck' with specific language to describe the actual taste. For example: 'This is an interesting taste called 'sweet'. Can you think of another food that is sweet?'

5. Repeat with the sour, bitter, spicy, salty and umami egg cups.

6. At this point, you could go straight into the 'Hugh's hair salad' recipe on page 64 of this book, to consolidate and demonstrate how these tastes can be mixed to add flavour to our food.

And another idea:

▶ Explore language to describe the textures of foods by setting up an activity with examples of different textures of foods, such as crisp, crunchy, chewy, hard, soft, rough, smooth, and juicy.

Where is this food from?

Focus

Understanding the world in terms of where the food that we eat comes from.

Skills

Sorting food items into animal or plant groups and matching images of where each food comes from.

What you need:

▶ Two tables: one labelled 'animal' and the other labelled 'plant'

▶ On the animal table: A4 colour pictures of a cow, sheep, chicken, pig, and either the ocean or a fish

▶ On the plant table: A4 colour pictures of an apple tree, wheat field, raspberry plant, plum tree, courgette plant, sweetcorn plant, pea pod, potato plant, and tomato plant

- A bag filled with safe food packaging (no sharp edges), models of food, or images of food, to represent:

  - ▷ Fish fingers and canned tuna
  - ▷ Roast chicken and eggs
  - ▷ Roast lamb and lamb kebabs
  - ▷ Sausages
  - ▷ Beef meatballs or burgers
  - ▷ Cheese and yoghurt
  - ▷ Bread and pasta

  - ▷ Various fruits, e.g. apples, plums, raspberries, tomatoes
  - ▷ Potatoes
  - ▷ A variety of vegetables, e.g. courgettes, peas, sweetcorn (fresh on the cob, and canned)

What you do:

1. Ask the children to think about where our food comes from before it arrives at a shop or market. Work towards the message that the food that we eat has come from either an animal or a plant.

2. Show the children the 'animal' and 'plant' tables, asking them to name the animals and plants in the pictures.

3. Show them the bag containing the food packaging/food models/food images. Ask the children to take turns in pulling an item from the bag. Ask them to name the food. Does it come from a plant or an animal?

4. With the support of the group, ask each child in turn to take their food item to the relevant animal or plant table, and match it with an image of the food source. For example, a bag of pasta would be placed with the picture of a wheat field. Continue with the rest of the food items in the bag.

And another idea:

- ▶ Try growing cress or herbs, or even pea shoots, indoors; and try growing tomatoes or potatoes in containers outdoors. The produce can be used in cooking activities.

- ▶ Try setting up a digging and planting role-play station, using a sand table filled with compost, buried potatoes and root vegetables, sequins as seeds, small trowels, plastic hand rakes and small toy tractors.

- ▶ Visit a farm, dairy, allotment, farmers market, greengrocers, butchers, fishmongers or bakery to further explore where our food comes from.

- ▶ Sing the nursery rhyme 'Oats and Beans and Barley Grow'.

Ready to cook?

Focus

Introduce an important aspect of food safety and hygiene through building a routine for getting ready to cook.

Skills

Following actions on a checklist; thinking about our own bodies and hygiene.

What you need:

▶ Prepare in advance a pictorial checklist poster (laminated if possible), with supporting sentences for the steps needed to get ready to cook:

  ▷ Tie long hair back.

  ▷ Take off any jewellery.

  ▷ Roll up long sleeves.

  ▷ Put on cooking aprons.

  ▷ Wash and dry hands.

▶ A doll with long hair, long sleeves, and something to use as an apron; also a hair band and bracelet, and a washing bowl and paper towels.

What you do:

1. Ask the children to share their ideas of things we need to do to get ready to cook.

2. Show the children the 'ready to cook?' checklist poster. Ask them what each step is. Question 'why?': for example, why do we need to tie long hair back?

3. Once the children are familiar with the 'ready to cook?' checklist, show them the doll, and explain that they need to help her to get ready to cook. Use the checklist to support the children in taking steps to tie back the doll's hair, take off the bracelet, roll up the long sleeves, put the apron on, and wash and dry her hands. The poster checklist can be used as a reminder before each cooking session in your setting.

4. Ask the children to get themselves ready to cook, which will consolidate the learning.

5. Prepare one of the recipes in this book.

And another idea:

▶   Set up the role-play area in your setting as a kitchen or café, with a selection of safe cooking equipment, washing bowls, aprons and the 'ready to cook?' checklist poster.

Recipes

Square porridge

Starter activities

Set up a sorting exploration activity by filling your water tray with plastic, wooden and craft-foam geometric shapes (some shapes will sink and others will float), and small plastic counting bears in different colours. Invite the children to identify the shapes and colours and sort them into groups using mini fishing nets and plastic scoops. Read a 'Goldilocks and the Three Bears' picture book with the children, and then make 'square porridge' together for a shape-themed bears' breakfast!

Focus

This recipe takes familiar breakfast ingredients and presents them as a tray bake. This is a great opportunity to talk with the children about the importance of eating breakfast and getting your 5-a-day.

Skills

Measuring, weighing, mashing, and mixing.

What you need:

Ingredients

▷ 160g porridge oats

▷ 100g plain flour

▷ 120g dried cherries

▷ 55g ground almonds

▷ 2 medium overripe bananas (brown skin)

▷ 250ml standard or reduced fat evaporated milk (unsweetened)

▷ 1 large egg

▷ 25g flaked almonds

Equipment

▷ Large mixing bowl, and dessert spoons

▷ Dinner plate, damp tea towel, and masher

▷ Large measuring jug, and forks

▷ Weighing scales

▷ Sharp kitchen knife (for adult use) or cookie cutters in various shapes (e.g. square, triangle, circle)

▷ 23cm/9" non-stick square tray-bake tin, and oven gloves

▷ Oven preheated to fan 180°C/350°F/Gas 4

What you do:

1. Ask the children to help weigh the dry ingredients (porridge oats, plain flour, dried cherries and ground almonds). If using balance scales, ask them if you need more or less for the scales to balance. The children can tip each weighed dry ingredient into the large mixing bowl and stir.

2. Place the dinner plate onto the damp tea towel to form a steady base for the children to mash the bananas onto. They could have a plate and a masher each, or could take turns to do some banana mashing.

3. Measure the evaporated milk in a large measuring jug. You could use a washable pen to mark the target volume on the outside of the jug so it is clearly visible to the children, and ask them to tell you when you have measured enough.

4. One child can help crack the egg into the large jug by gently tapping the egg onto the table then holding it over the jug and breaking it open using both thumbs. Tap, tap, and crack!

5. Another child can scoop the mashed banana into the jug and then all the children can take turns to mix it thoroughly with a fork.

6. Ask one child to tip the jug of wet ingredients into the bowl of dry ingredients. The children can take turns gently mixing to combine the ingredients.

7. Empty this into the square tray-bake tin. Ask the children to gently jiggle the tin until the mixture has spread out flat.

8. Ask the children to sprinkle the top with flaked almonds.

9. Bake in the preheated oven for 30 minutes, or until the top is lightly golden.

10. Leave to cool, then cut into 16 small squares using a sharp kitchen knife. Alternatively, you could turn out the tray bake onto a chopping board or mat and use different geometric shape cookie cutters to make triangles, circles, or rectangles.

And another idea:

▶ Experiment with different dried fruits, such as chopped dried apricots, raisins, sultanas, or even dried strawberries. For an occasional treat, stir in some chocolate chips, or spice it up by adding half a teaspoon of cinnamon or mixed spice. Try cutting into fingers to dip into fromage frais.

▶ Set up an activity with coloured wooden pattern blocks or craft-foam shapes. Encourage the children to identify the shapes and use them to make a bear picture.

▶ Try a porridge play dough activity to explore textures and shape by kneading uncooked porridge oats into play dough. Set out a selection of bear and geometric shape cookie cutters, extra porridge oats for sprinkling and rolling pins.

▶ Sing 'Teddy Bear's Picnic' or 'Teddy Bear, Teddy Bear, Turn Around' and learn the actions together.

▶ Read 'We're Going on a Bear Hunt' by Michael Rosen.

Jungle cakes

Starter activities

Explore the jungle by setting up your role-play area with large leaves, a wide range of jungle animal soft toys, jungle minibeast figures, large painted cardboard palm trees and bunches of bananas, and play jungle sounds on speakers. Look at a globe with the children and talk about the different parts of the world where jungles are found, the different people and animals that live there, and what the weather is like. Read 'The Tiger Who Came to Tea' by Judith Kerr and then make Jungle Cakes together for the tiger!

Focus

These simple little cakes use wholemeal flour. Fruit is a great way of providing sweetness in place of sugar, which can be linked back to the Eatwell Plate healthy eating messages. This recipe makes 10 cakes.

Skills

Weighing, measuring, mashing, mixing and scooping.

What you need:

Ingredients

- ▷ 50g wholemeal self-raising flour
- ▷ 50g white self-raising flour
- ▷ 1/2 teaspoon ground cinnamon
- ▷ 3 tablespoons vegetable/rapeseed oil
- ▷ 3 medium overripe bananas (brown skin)
- ▷ 1 large egg

Equipment

- ▷ Small and large mixing bowls
- ▷ Sieves and weighing scales
- ▷ Dinner plate, damp tea towel and masher
- ▷ Measuring spoons, wooden spoons, teaspoons, forks and whisks
- ▷ 12-hole bun tin lined with 10 paper baking cases
- ▷ Oven gloves and wire wrack
- ▷ Oven preheated to fan 180°C/350°F/Gas 4

What you do:

1. Ask the children to help weigh the flour and sift into a large mixing bowl. Balance scales can help children learning to add more or take away until the target weight is reached.

2. Show the children how to use the measuring spoons to measure the cinnamon and mix into the flour.

3. Ask one child to gently tap the egg on the table. Then hold it over a small mixing bowl and crack it open using both thumbs. Tap, tap, and crack! The children can then take turns to whisk the egg with a fork or whisk.

4. Show the children how to use the measuring spoons to measure the oil and add it to the egg mixture.

5. Place the dinner plate on top of the folded damp tea towel to prevent it slipping. Ask the children to help peel the bananas (you may need to start it for them) and mash them well on the plate until smooth. Add to the oil and egg and mix again.

6. Empty the small bowl of wet ingredients into the large bowl of dry ingredients and ask the children to take turns gently mixing until the flour is incorporated.

7. Show the children how to use two teaspoons to scoop and scrape the mixture into the baking cases. Use two heaped teaspoons in each of the 10 cases.

8. Bake in the preheated oven for about 15 minutes or until well risen, light golden and firm to touch.

9. Lift the cases out of the bun tin and cool on a wire rack.

And another idea:

▶ Decorate each cooled cake with a crunchy banana chip, stuck on with a blob of vanilla cream cheese. Try adding dried fruit, chopped nuts or even chocolate chips before baking; you could also try substituting 2 tablespoons of flour for 2 tablespoons of cocoa powder to make chocolate banana cakes. Bake in a greased mini muffin tin for extra visual appeal.

▶ Sing and dance to 'Down in the Jungle Where Nobody Goes'.

▶ Read 'Rumble in the Jungle' by Giles Andrea and look through a jungle animal picture reference book.

▶ Have a jungle animal drama session where the children use their bodies and voices to become different jungle animals.

▶ Go on a trip to a Zoo, Animal Sanctuary, Safari Park or Rescue Centre, where the children can see real jungle animals.

Fairy bread

Starter activities

Set up a 'fairy bakery' in your role-play area. Add a counter and shelves lined with baskets to display produce such as model cakes and breads. Decorate with flowers and make sparkly banners. Set out aprons and baker's hats, a cash register, and paper bags. You could use pouches of gemstones as money, or take the children outside to find treasure in nature to use as currency in the bakery. Then come together to make fairy bread.

Focus

This simple soda bread recipe is super quick to make and bake. It is a great introduction to bread making without any heavy kneading or long waits between stages. This can be linked back to the food groups in the Eatwell Plate. Makes 12 tiny fairy loaves.

Skills

Weighing, measuring, mashing, mixing and scooping.

What you need:

Ingredients

- ▷ 225g white self-raising flour
- ▷ 1/2 teaspoon salt
- ▷ 1/2 teaspoon bicarbonate of soda
- ▷ 200ml buttermilk
- ▷ 1 tablespoon of unsalted butter, melted

Equipment

- ▷ Large mixing bowls and sieves
- ▷ Dessert spoons and measuring spoons
- ▷ Greased mini muffin tin or a baking sheet lined with non-stick baking paper
- ▷ Oven gloves and wire wrack
- ▷ Pastry brush
- ▷ Oven preheated to fan 190°C/375°F/Gas 5

What you do:

1. Ask the children to help weigh out the flour, salt and bicarbonate of soda and then sift them into a large mixing bowl and take turns to mix well.

2. Show them how to dig out a well in the centre of the flour using a spoon. Then pour in the buttermilk.

3. The children can take turns to mix very gently with a dessert spoon just until the mixture comes together.

4. Ask the children to use gentle hands to pat the dough in the bowl so that it comes together into a ball. The key to light soda bread is to handle it as little as possible. However, this recipe uses self-raising flour to give an extra lift that should counteract any enthusiastic handling.

5. The children can take turns using a tablespoon measure to scoop out blobs of dough. These can be placed into a greased mini muffin tin or onto a lined baking sheet. This should make about 12 tiny fairy loaves.

6. Bake in the preheated oven for 10-12 minutes or until golden brown.

7. When they come out of the oven, brush the tops with a little melted butter and leave on a wire rack to cool.

And another idea:

▶ Use half wholemeal self-raising flour to increase the fibre, and try adding a tablespoon of mixed seeds to the dough and sprinkling a few seeds on top of the loaves before baking. For a touch of magic fairy dust, sprinkle the bread with edible glitter once cooled. You could also adapt the recipe to make fairy fruit buns by adding half a teaspoon of mixed spice and 2 tablespoons of currants to the dough.

▶ Read 'Little Red Hen' to explore where the ingredients for bread come from.

▶ Set up an art activity by giving the children fairy cake outlines printed on paper. They can then use pearlescent paint, glitter, glue, flowers, petals and acorn cups to make their own fairy cake designs.

▶ Set out glitter play dough with a selection of baking equipment and cupcake holders as an invitation for imaginative fairy bakery play.

▶ Make links with your local community by visiting a flourmill, bakery or bread market stall.

▶ In the summer months, try a welly walk to visit local farmland where wheat crops are growing.

Volcano dips

Starter activities

Have a dinosaur-themed sensory play session by whizzing red food colouring, washing up liquid and a little water in a blender to create foam lava. Add this to your water table or sand tray, along with a large conical funnel for a volcano, rocks, pebbles and dinosaur figures for small world play. Read a dinosaur picture book with the children, such as 'Dinosaur Roar' by Henrietta Stickland, to explore opposites. Then make volcano dips together.

Focus

This is an opportunity to prepare vegetables and pulses in a different way, with a variety of colours, flavours and textures. This links back to the Eatwell Plate and 5-a-day.

Skills

Weighing, measuring, grating, and mixing

What you need:

Ingredients for the tzatziki volcano dip
- ▷ 150g standard or fat-free Greek yoghurt
- ▷ 1/2 a cucumber, washed and sliced in two lengthways
- ▷ 1/2 a peeled clove of garlic, pressed
- ▷ 1 teaspoon lemon juice

Ingredients for the beetroot volcano dip
- ▷ 200g cooked vacuum packed beetroot, quartered (choose a variety without vinegar)
- ▷ 5 tablespoons standard or reduced fat soft cheese
- ▷ 2 teaspoons lemon juice
- ▷ 1/4 peeled clove of garlic, pressed
- ▷ 1/4 teaspoon ground cumin
- ▷ 1/4 teaspoon ground coriander seeds

Ingredients for the beany volcano dip
- ▷ 400g tin of haricot beans, drained and rinsed
- ▷ 2 tablespoons tahini paste
- ▷ 4 tablespoons lemon juice
- ▷ 1 teaspoon harissa paste
- ▷ 1 tablespoon sundried tomato paste
- ▷ 1 teaspoon extra virgin olive oil

Dippers
- ▷ Vegetable dippers such as carrot sticks, cucumber sticks, red pepper sticks, celery sticks, sugar snap peas and broccoli florets.
- ▷ Starchy dippers such as bread sticks, toast dippers shaped with dinosaur cookie cutters, or even 'boulders' made with the 'fairy bread' recipe in this book.

Equipment
- ▷ Large mixing bowl and sieve
- ▷ Grater (rotary graters that fix securely onto the table can be helpful for involving young children)
- ▷ Hand blender and beakers (if you don't have 2 of each, rinse in between dips)
- ▷ Garlic press
- ▷ Dessert spoons, measuring spoons and teaspoons
- ▷ Vegetable knife and chopping board
- ▷ Serving bowls, cups and transparent cups

What you do:

Tzatziki volcano dip

1. Show the children how to use a teaspoon to scrape the seeds out of the cucumber. Discard the seeds.

2. Grate the cucumber. The children can get involved in this by using a rotary grater. This can work well in pairs with one child applying pressure and the other child turning the handle. Place the grated cucumber in a sieve and leave it to drain over a bowl.

3. Add the Greek yoghurt to a serving bowl. Add the lemon juice and pressed garlic and the children can take turns to mix well.

4. Show the children how to use the back of a cup to press the juice out of the grated cucumber in the sieve. Take time to squeeze out as much liquid as possible, then the children can add the drained cucumber to the yoghurt and mix well. Leave to stand for a few minutes whilst the flavours develop.

Beetroot volcano dip

1. Support the children in weighing and measuring the beetroot, soft cheese, garlic, lemon juice, ground cumin and ground coriander seed and add to the blender beaker.

2. The children can watch you use the hand blender to blend the ingredients until smooth. This is a good opportunity to talk about safety around sharp equipment.

3. Remove the blade so the children can use a spoon to scrape the dip into a serving bowl.

Beany volcano dip

1. Support the children in measuring the drained haricot beans, tahini, lemon juice, harissa paste, sundried tomato paste and oil and add to the blender beaker.

2. The children can watch you use the hand blender to blend the ingredients until smooth.

3. Remove the blade so the children can use a spoon to scrape the dip into a serving bowl.

Serve with a selection of the dippers suggested above.

And another idea:

▶ Ask the children each to put 1-2 tablespoons of their favourite dip into their own transparent cup. Then fill the cups with vegetable sticks for a portable snack to take outdoors.

▶ Try experimenting with fresh or dry herbs such as mint or dill in the tzatziki, or basil in the beany dip.

▶ Try adding any of the dips to a pitta pocket with salad and falafel.

▶ Make dinosaur bones with the children out of salt dough and bake on a low heat until dried out and hard. Bury the dinosaur bones in the sandpit and encourage the children to do some Palaeontologist role-play by uncovering the bones using small trowels and brushes.

▶ Ask the children to put a range of dinosaur figures into size order as a maths activity.

▶ Set up a finger writing sand tray using a tray and green or brown sand. Decorate with small pebbles and mini dinosaur figures. This can be used for mark making, tracing letters or sight words, depending on the ages and stages of the children.

▶ Visit a museum with a dinosaur exhibition.

Moon rock muffins

Starter activities

Investigate the moon with an interactive demonstration. Show the children a large, detailed photo of the moon. What can they see? Discuss the impact craters made by solid objects such as asteroids or meteorites crashing into the surface of the moon. Mix grey powdered paint with flour in the sand tray. Then, ask the children to scrunch up foil into different sized balls to drop into the flour and create their own lunar landscape full of impact craters. Then make moon rock muffins together.

Focus

This recipe uses a familiar process and introduces vegetable and savoury flavours. These are ideal for snack time. Makes 6 muffins.

Skills

Measuring, weighing, sifting, grating, and mixing

What you need:

Ingredients

▷ 50g wholemeal self-raising flour

▷ 50g white self-raising flour

▷ 1/2 teaspoon mustard powder

▷ 1 large egg

▷ 120ml semi-skimmed milk

▷ 60g mature cheddar cheese (standard or reduced fat)

▷ 100g peeled carrots

Equipment

▷ Small and large mixing bowls

▷ Sieves and weighing scales

▷ Grater (rotary graters that fix securely onto the table can be helpful for involving young children)

▷ Measuring spoons, wooden spoons, teaspoons, forks and whisks

▷ 12-hole muffin tin, well-greased

▷ Oven gloves and wire wrack

▷ Oven preheated to fan 180°C/350°F/Gas 4

What you do:

1. Ask the children to help weigh the flour and sift into a large mixing bowl. Balance scales can help children learn to add more or take away until the target weight is reached.

2. Show the children how to use the measuring spoons to measure the mustard powder and mix into the flour.

3. One child can help crack the egg into the small mixing bowl by gently tapping the egg onto the table then holding it over the bowl and breaking it open using both thumbs. Tap, tap, and crack! Add the milk to the egg and ask the children to take turns whisking with a fork or whisk.

4. Show the children how to dig a well in the flour with a spoon and pour in the small bowl of wet ingredients. The children can take turns to gently mix until the flour is incorporated.

5. The children can help weigh out the cheese and carrots, and then pass through the rotary grater. This can work well in pairs with one child applying pressure and the other child turning the handle. Mix the grated carrot and cheese into the muffin batter.

6. Show the children how to use two teaspoons to scoop and scrape the mixture evenly into the greased muffin tin. The mixture should be enough for 6 muffins.

7. Bake in the preheated oven for about 20 to 25 minutes or until the muffins are well-risen, golden brown, and firm to touch.

8. After cooling for 5 minutes, use a teaspoon to gently lift the muffins out of the tin and leave to cool on a wire rack.

And another idea:

▶ Try grated courgette instead of carrot. Also try adding a heaped tablespoon of sunflower seeds to the batter and sprinkle a few on top of the muffins before baking.

▶ Create a moon dust finger-writing tray with grey decorative sand and a shiny disposable foil tray. This can be used for mark making, tracing letters or sight words depending on the age and stage.

▶ Sing songs with the children, such as 'Zoom Zoom Zoom, We're Going to the Moon' and 'Twinkle, Twinkle, Little Star'.

▶ Read moon themed picture books with the children, such as 'Man on the Moon' by Simon Bartram and 'Whatever Next!' by Jill Murphy.

▶ Visit a play park for an astronaut physical training session with exercises, obstacle courses, and g-force practice on the park spinning apparatus.

▶ Visit a science museum with a space or moon exhibition.

Ready-base pizza

Starter activities

Make simple pizza jigsaw puzzles using paper plates. The children can draw on their own toppings using pens or paint. Help them to draw lines using a ruler and pen to divide their pizzas into slices. Support them in using scissors to cut along the lines. Then they can take apart and put back together their pizza puzzles. They can also be used for simple subtraction activities. Then make your own ready-base pizzas!

Focus

Preparing pizza can be a popular way to involve children in preparing their own vegetable dish. This can be linked back to the healthy eating messages in the Eatwell Plate and 5 A Day. Makes enough for 6 to share.

Skills

Measuring, scooping, spooning, mixing, spreading, snipping, sprinkling, and grating.

What you need:

Ingredients

 ▷ 100g tomato puree
 ▷ 50g sundried tomato paste
 ▷ 1 peeled clove of garlic, pressed
 ▷ 1 teaspoon dried oregano
 ▷ 4 wholemeal flatbread wraps (2 rectangular flatbread wraps usually fit nicely onto one baking tray)
 ▷ 2 spring onions, washed
 ▷ 1/2 red pepper, washed and finely diced. Leave the remaining half out for the children to explore, plus a few thin strips of pepper for them to snip
 ▷ 198g tin of sweetcorn with no added salt or sugar, drained
 ▷ 100g grated cheddar or mozzarella cheese (standard or reduced fat)

Equipment

 ▷ Small mixing bowl, dessert spoons, teaspoons and measuring spoons
 ▷ Garlic press, silicone spatula, box grater or rotary grater
 ▷ Mugs and clean nursery scissors, reserved for kitchen use only
 ▷ Kitchen scissors or pizza slice
 ▷ 2 non-stick baking sheets or shallow-sided baking trays
 ▷ Oven preheated to fan 220°C/475°F/Gas 9

What you do:

1. Show the children how to measure out the tomato puree, sundried tomato paste, pressed garlic and dried oregano and add to a small mixing bowl. The children can take turns to mix well.

2. Place the flat breads onto the baking sheets and divide the tomato mixture between them. Show the children how they can use the back of a teaspoon or a silicone spatula to spread out the tomato mixture to cover the flatbreads.

3. The children can carefully snip the spring onions into a mug, and sprinkle over the pizzas.

4. The children can use their scissors to snip the red pepper strips and add this to the remaining finely diced red pepper, then sprinkle over the pizzas.

5. Ask the children to sprinkle the sweetcorn over the pizzas. You may not need all of it, as you don't want the pizzas to be overloaded.

6. Finally, they can sprinkle over the cheese. This will hold the rest of the toppings in place.

7. Bake in the preheated oven for 5-7 minutes or until the peppers have softened and the cheese is bubbling.

8. Leave to cool before using kitchen scissors or a pizza slice to cut into smaller serving sizes.

And another idea:

▶ Experiment with different toppings, such as diced cooked chicken and torn up mushrooms, ham and pineapple chunks, chunks of tinned tuna and sliced olives, or any roasted vegetables. Just avoid overloading as this can lead to a soggy pizza!

▶ Experiment with different ready bases, such as English muffins, toast, pitta, roti, chapatti, or tortilla wraps.

▶ This recipe can be adapted to themes easily. For example, before adding the toppings, cut the pizzas into heart shapes (fold and snip) for Valentine's Day. Try bagel pizzas with red and green toppings for Christmas wreaths.

▶ Read books involving a pizza theme, such as 'Pizza for Pirates' by Adam and Charlotte Guillain or 'Pizza Kittens' by Charlotte Voake.

▶ Set up a play-dough pizzeria with natural colour play dough, found/fallen natural object toppings, and plastic rotary pizza cutters.

▶ Have a pizza themed geometric shapes activity with pizza outlines on paper and toppings to cut and stick, such as squares of ham, rectangles of pineapple, triangles of pepper and circles of pepperoni. This could be adapted to a colours or counting session, too.

Bread crust nests

Starter activities

Try a bird's nest role-play activity as part of a Spring or Easter theme. Create the nest using chunky cushions or boxes, and cover with a brown sheet. Give the children bird-beak masks and set out boxes full of straw or shredded paper and feathers for them to line their nest with. Provide small plastic eggs and toy chicks. A grass-effect rug covered with pipe-cleaner worms could be used for feeding the chicks during the role-play! Then make bread crust nests together.

Focus

The children can prepare their own healthy savoury snack. Once mastered, they can use this as a starting point for dreaming up their own favourite fillings.

Skills

Cutting, rolling, spreading, grating, sprinkling, mixing, pouring, and shapes.

What you need:

Ingredients

- ▷ 6 slices of thick cut wholemeal bread
- ▷ Olive spread
- ▷ 20g mature cheddar cheese (standard or reduced fat)
- ▷ 3 cherry tomatoes, halved
- ▷ 3 large eggs

Equipment

- ▷ 98mm circle scone cutters (or any round cutter that fits just inside the crust of a slice of bread)
- ▷ Rolling pins, reserved for kitchen use only
- ▷ Butter knives
- ▷ Grater (rotary graters that fix securely to the table can be helpful for involving young children)
- ▷ Weighing scales
- ▷ Large jug and fork or whisk
- ▷ Muffin tin
- ▷ Cooling rack
- ▷ Oven gloves
- ▷ Oven preheated to fan 180°C/350°F/Gas 4

What you do:

1. Support the children in using the circle scone cutters to cut out a circle from each slice of bread. Ideally, this should come as close to the edge as possible, leaving just the crusts behind. Keep the crusts for breadcrumbs and freeze for future use.

2. Next, ask the children to use their rolling pins to flatten down their bread circles.

3. Support them in using a butter knife to spread the olive spread over one side of each bread circle.

4. Each bread circle can then be gently tucked butter-side down into the muffin tray cups to form six bread nests.

5. Involve the children in grating the cheese using a rotary grater. This can work well in pairs, with one child applying pressure and the other child turning the handle. Divide the grated cheese between the six bread nests.

6. Ask the children to put one cherry tomato half, cut side up, into each bread nest.

7. Show the children how to gently tap an egg on the table. Then hold it over the jug and crack it open using both thumbs. Tap, tap, and crack! Add three eggs in total to the jug then ask the children to take turns to whisk.

8. Divide the egg mixture between the six bread cups, being careful not to overfill.

9. Bake in the preheated oven for 15-20 minutes or until the egg is light golden.

10. Lift each bread crust nest out with a teaspoon and leave to cool on a wire rack.

And another idea:

▶ Encourage the children to make this recipe their own by dreaming up their favourite ingredients to add before pouring in the egg mixture. Offer a selection of ingredients to experiment with, such as chives, spring onions, sweetcorn, canned tuna, diced mushrooms, chopped ham, or peas. You could add more flavour to the whisked egg by mixing in 1/4 teaspoon of ground black pepper or paprika.

▶ Try an Easter egg design activity by cutting out large egg shapes from coloured card. The children can then decorate their eggs with different coloured or patterned masking tape. Cut different lengths of the tape and stick to the edge of a table for easier access. Encourage the children to experiment with snipping, scrunching and tearing.

▶ Look into whether someone in your local community could donate an abandoned empty bird's nest (from a past breeding season) for the children to have a close look at.

▶ Arrange a visit from a wildlife or bird charity children's educator.

▶ Set up a pattern sequencing activity with different coloured mini chicks and mini plastic eggs (available in many shops close to Easter time).

Stuffed jackets

Starter activities

Set up a potato harvest activity as part of a 'where food comes from', seasonal or harvest theme. Bury potatoes in compost in the sand table and add small-world tractors, trowels, brushes and small buckets for harvesting play. Once the children have found all of the potatoes, they can place them in large tubs of warm water and clean them with vegetable scrubbing brushes and dry with tea towels. Then make stuffed jackets together.

Focus

This recipe is a great basis for incorporating vegetables into a meal. It is easily customised to include different vegetable combinations. Makes six half jackets.

Skills

Mashing, scooping, grating, weighing, mixing, and transferring.

What you need:

Ingredients

▷ 3 small baked potatoes, cooled (bake up to 2 days in advance, then cover and refrigerate)

▷ 75g cooked broccoli, cooled (cook until tender enough to mash, up to 2 days in advance and then refrigerate)

▷ 75g cooked cauliflower, cooled (cook until tender enough to mash, up to 2 days in advance and then refrigerate)

▷ 60g cheddar cheese (standard or reduced fat)

▷ 1/4 teaspoon ground black pepper

▷ 1 teaspoon Worcestershire sauce

▷ 3 tablespoons crème fraiche (standard or half fat)

Equipment

▷ Teaspoons, dessert spoons and measuring spoons

▷ Large mixing bowl, potato masher and forks

▷ Weighing scales, rotary grater that fixes securely to the table and a vegetable knife

▷ Shallow bun tray and oven gloves

▷ Oven preheated to fan 180°C/350°F/Gas 4

What you do:

1. Cut the baked potatoes in half.

2. Support the children in using teaspoons to gently scoop out the potato flesh, leaving the skins unbroken. Add the potato flesh to the large mixing bowl.

3. Nestle the 6 potato skins into a shallow bun tray to stop them tipping.

4. Ask the children to add the cooked broccoli and cauliflower to the mixing bowl with the potato flesh. They can take turns using the masher to mash thoroughly.

5. Show the children how to grate the cheese with the rotary grater. This can work well in pairs with one child applying pressure and the other child turning the handle.

6. Add the grated cheese to the mixing bowl and support the children in measuring and adding the black pepper, Worcestershire sauce, and crème fraiche. The children can take turns to mix this well to form the potato stuffing mixture.

7. Fill the potato skins with the stuffing mixture. Show the children how to use the back of a spoon to pack it down and heap more on top.

8. Bake in the preheated oven for 15 minutes.

And another idea:

▶ Experiment with different fillings, such as sweetcorn and diced red pepper, peas and tuna, or even drained baked beans. Snip in fresh herbs and spring onions for extra flavour. Try the recipe using sweet potatoes with sweetcorn, diced red pepper and a teaspoon of Mexican taco spice mix.

▶ Grow potatoes in your outdoor space, in containers, or even in a 2L clear drinks bottle with the top cut off and drainage holes for easy observation.

▶ Visit a local allotment and arrange for the children to help the community to dig up potatoes when they are ready to harvest.

▶ Sing 'One Potato, Two Potato, Three Potato, Four', using real potatoes as props for a counting activity.

▶ Read 'Supertato' by Sue Hendra.

▶ Try an art activity using a selection of different patterned potato stamps (some wavy lines, some grids, some triangular, etc.). Fill dishes with different colour paints and the children can then use the potato stamps to print with. This makes great wrapping paper.

Crispy salmon balls

Starter activities

Set up an ocean and fish themed literacy activity. Use a blue paddling pool and coloured card cut-out fish shapes, each marked with a letter on the body. Use split pins for eyes, and set out magnetic fishing rods. Depending on the ages and stages of the children, they could name the letter sound each time they catch a fish, or try to catch the letters they need to spell their name. Then make crispy salmon balls.

Focus

This recipe is a great basis for incorporating vegetables into a meal. Tinned pink salmon counts as an oily fish and is a great ingredient to introduce young children to preparing their own fish dish. Makes 10-12 small balls.

Skills

Crushing, measuring, weighing, mixing, snipping, scooping, shaping, and coating.

What you need:

Ingredients

▷ 85g cornflakes (look at the ingredients label and select a variety with a lower salt content)

▷ 1 large egg

▷ 1 teaspoon oil (olive/vegetable/rapeseed)

▷ 1/4 teaspoon ground black pepper

▷ Zest of 1 unwaxed lemon

▷ 6 chives

▷ 2 teaspoons of sundried tomato paste

▷ 170g tin of skinless and boneless pink salmon, drained. You can use tinned salmon with bones, which is a great source of calcium. However, you would need to pass it through a blender first until smooth.

Equipment

▷ Medium zip lock food storage bags and cups

▷ Small bowls and large mixing bowls

▷ Dessert spoons, measuring spoons and forks

▷ Zester, tin opener and oven gloves

▷ Baking sheet lined with non-stick baking paper

▷ Oven preheated to fan 190°C/375°F/Gas 5

What you do:

1. Ask the children to help weigh the cornflakes. Balance scales can help children learn to add more or take away until the target weight is reached. Tip the cornflakes into the zip lock food storage bag, press out the air and then zip closed.

2. Ask the children to take turns crushing the cornflakes with their hands or by pressing with cups until sandy. Tip into a small bowl and set aside.

3. Ask one child to gently tap the egg on the table. Then hold it over a small mixing bowl and crack it open using both thumbs. Tap, tap, and crack!

4. The children can take turns whisking the egg. Then measure and add the pepper, oil, lemon zest, sundried tomato paste and mix.

5. Add the salmon to the mixing bowl and show the children how to break it up with the back of a fork.

6. The children can snip in the chives and add 8 tablespoons of the crushed cornflakes. Mix well.

7. Show the children how to scoop out a tablespoon of the mixture and squash it into a ball with their hands. Roll the ball in the bowl of crushed cornflakes to coat and place it on the lined baking sheet. Repeat with the remaining mixture. This should make 10-12 balls.

8. Bake in the preheated oven for 10-15 minutes and cool a little before serving.

And another idea:

▶ Try adding 1-2 tablespoons of sweetcorn or finely diced red pepper to the mixture before rolling into balls.

▶ Experiment with different herbs such as dill or parsley.

▶ This recipe works just as well with tuna tinned in water.

▶ Try an ocean themed sensory small world activity. Fill the water tray with blue jelly (powdered gelatine, hot water and blue food colouring according to packet instructions) or blue water beads. Add some water to loosen, small world ocean creature figures, shells, slotted spoons and mini nets.

▶ Read fish themed books such as' The Rainbow Fish' by Marcus Pfister or 'Hooray for Fish' by Lucy Cousins.

▶ Try a matching pairs activity using sea creature picture cards.

▶ Add sand to play dough and mark letters or numbers on small shells. Let the children play and create. They might stick on their name using the shells or decorate with colourful fish tank gravel and fish tank plastic seaweed.

Root chips

Starter activities

Try a harvest themed activity. Fill the sand table with dark brown decorative sand or dyed brown rice. 'Plant' a selection of seasonal ripe root vegetables into the sand table, preferably including a few with green tops (such as carrots). Add mini trowels, hand forks and a few small world rabbits and small plant pots. As they discover the vegetables, talk with them about root vegetables: discuss which parts grow above and below the ground, what their names are, and whether the children have eaten them before. Then make root chips.

Focus

Preparing potatoes and root vegetables in the familiar format of a chip. The chopping is quite advanced in this recipe, so you may want to prepare in advance or support the safe use of a potato chipper.

Skills

Measuring, coating, and spreading.

What you need:

Ingredients

▷ 100g potato cut into approximately 1cm by 5cm chips

▷ 90g carrot, cut into 5cm lengths, then halved lengthwise, then cut into thirds to form wedge chips

▷ 70g parsnip, cut into approximately 2cm by 5cm chips as these cook quicker (cut around the core)

▷ 80g sweet potato, cut into approximately 2cm by 5cm chips as these cook quicker

▷ 1 tablespoon olive oil

▷ 1/4 teaspoon ground black pepper

▷ 1/2 teaspoon sweet paprika

Equipment

▷ Chopping board, vegetable knife, potato peeler and possibly a potato chipper

▷ Measuring spoons and slotted spatula

▷ Medium zip-lock food bag

▷ Baking tray lined with non-stick baking paper

▷ Oven gloves

▷ Oven preheated to fan 180°C/350°F/Gas 4

What you do:

1. Prepare the potatoes and root vegetables into chip shapes, either in advance or with the children using a safe method potato chipper. Have whole potatoes and root vegetables on display on the table so that the children can see where each chip has come from.

2. Ask the children to put all of the chipped potatoes and root vegetables into the zip-lock bag. Then show them how to use the measuring spoons to add the olive oil, black pepper, and paprika.

3. Close the zip-lock bag and ask the children to take turns shaking, rubbing, and scrunching the bag until the chips are well coated.

4. Tip the chips onto the lined baking tray, spread out, and bake in the preheated oven for 30 minutes. Turn over half way if possible for even colour.

And another idea:

▶ Experiment with other root vegetables in addition to the potatoes, such as beetroot, swede, turnips, yams or celeriac. Try adding rosemary leaves and a few garlic cloves (skin on) to add more flavour.

▶ Sing and dance to songs such as 'Dingle Dangle Scarecrow' and 'Sleeping Bunnies'.

▶ Visit a community allotment or vegetable farm and arrange for the children to get hands on in the physical work of harvesting with appropriately sized tools.

▶ Read picture books such as 'Oliver's Vegetables' by Vivian French or a harvest time picture book.

▶ Arrange for the children to get involved with any harvest celebrations happening in your community and make wider links to harvest celebrations in different religions or different parts of the world.

Hugh's hair salad

Starter activities

Set up a hairdresser role-play activity as part of a personal care theme. Use chairs and mirrors, cardboard cut-out scissors, hair brushes, donated hair dryers (cords removed), rollers, empty shampoo bottles, gowns, towels, dolls with hair, dustpans and brushes. Talk with the children about how they care for their own hair. Read 'Hugh Shampoo' by Karen George and then make Hugh's hair salad.

Focus

This recipe can follow directly on from the Wake Up, Taste Buds! activity on page 27 of this book. This is a fun way for the children to assemble their own balanced meal.

Skills

Scooping, measuring, whisking, snapping, mixing, and language surrounding tastes.

What you need:

Ingredients

▶ 5 small egg cups per child, containing examples of different tastes:

  ▷ Sweet: 1 teaspoon of honey

  ▷ Sour: 1 teaspoon of lemon juice

  ▷ Bitter: small pinch of lemon zest

  ▷ Salty and Umami: 1/2 teaspoon of soy sauce

  ▷ Spicy: 1/4 teaspoon of minced ginger

▶ 1/2 to 1 small cup of cooked and rinsed fine noodles

▶ 3 sugar snap peas per child

▶ 3 baby sweetcorn cobs per child

▶ 2 tablespoons per child of either diced cooked chicken/beef/pork, cooked prawns, well-cooked scrambled egg, or cooked soya/edamame beans

▶ 1/2 teaspoon oil (vegetable or rapeseed) per child

Equipment

  ▷ Cereal bowls, forks, mini whisks

  ▷ Teaspoons and measuring spoons

What you do:

1. Talk to the children about how we can mix different tastes together to add flavour to our food.

2. Ask the children to empty all five of their egg cups into their own cereal bowl. Talk whilst they work, for example: 'First let's add something sweet', then 'Now let's add something sour', and so on.

3. Ask the children to add 1/2 a teaspoon of oil to each cereal bowl. They can use a mini whisk to thoroughly combine to create a dressing.

4. Tip 1/2 to 1 small cup of cooked and rinsed fine noodles into each child's cereal bowl.

5. Then ask them to break up their sugar snap peas and baby sweetcorn cobs and add to their noodles.

6. Lastly, add the protein (cooked chicken/beef/pork, cooked prawns, scrambled egg or soya/edamame beans) and show the children how to use two forks to mix and cover the noodles in the dressing.

7. Taste and encourage the children to use describing words.

And another idea:

▶ Try adding half a teaspoon of Chinese 5 Spice to the dressing.

▶ You could set this up as a pick and mix activity, using a poster of the Eatwell Plate with a variety of ingredient options set on top of the relevant food groups. Then, guide the children in choosing servings from the starchy, protein, and vegetable food groups to add to their bowl and create their own favourite salad.

▶ During circle time, encourage the children to talk about their own hair care (washing, brushing, combing, hair cuts, hair bands, braiding etc.). Talk about the similarities and differences, and likes and dislikes.

▶ Try a hair cutting play dough activity by asking the children to use an extruder to make play dough hair and practice scissor skills.

▶ Use hair care objects such as empty shampoo bottles, brushes or combs and ask the children to count, try some addition or subtraction, sort into size order or do colour matching activities.

Quesadillas

Starter activities

Try a Mexican theme to explore foods from different parts of the world. Look at Mexico on a globe, show the children the Mexican flag, and talk about how different types of beans and corn are part of the Mexican diet. Set up a 'Mexican street-food vendor' role-play area with a counter, colourful tarpaulin, a sign, a large silver foil disposable circular platter to use as hot plate, paper plates for tortillas, small fabric pieces or tissue paper to use as fillings, empty catering sauce bottles, aprons, caps, and baskets of fresh fruit. Then make quesadillas together.

Focus

This Mexican style snack or main meal is well balanced and is a great way of tasting vegetables and beans. Makes six mini quesadillas.

Skills

Measuring, mixing, grating, snipping, scooping and folding. Using measuring cups as an alternative method to weighing scales.

What you need:

Ingredients

- ▷ 1 cup of tomato based salsa (ready made or homemade)
- ▷ 1 teaspoon ground cumin
- ▷ 1/2 teaspoon smoked paprika
- ▷ 1 cup tinned black beans, drained and rinsed
- ▷ 1 cup tinned sweetcorn (no added sugar or salt), drained
- ▷ 2 cups cheddar cheese (standard or reduced fat)
- ▷ 2 spring onions
- ▷ 4 sprigs of coriander
- ▷ 6 mini tortilla wraps

Equipment

- ▷ 2 baking sheets, lined with non-stick baking paper
- ▷ Oven gloves
- ▷ Large mixing bowl
- ▷ Masher and rotary grater that fixes securely to the table
- ▷ Clean nursery scissors used for cooking only
- ▷ Dessert spoons, measuring spoons, and a set of measuring cups
- ▷ Oven preheated to fan 180°C/350°F/Gas 4

What you do:

1. Ask the children to add half of the black beans to a large mixing bowl and take turns to crush them with the masher.
2. Show them how to measure and add the salsa, cumin and smoked paprika to the crushed black beans and mix with a dessert spoon.
3. Ask them to add the remaining black beans and sweetcorn.
4. Weigh the cheese and show the children how to add it to the rotary grater. This can work well in pairs with one child applying pressure and the other child turning the handle. Add the grated cheese to the beans.
5. Support the children in using scissors to carefully snip the spring onion into the bowl.
6. Ask them to tear in the coriander leaves and snip in the stalks.
7. The children can take turns mixing the ingredients together. This will form the filling.

8. Ask the children to place 2 heaped tablespoons of filling onto each mini tortilla wrap. They can then fold each wrap in half and gently press down to form the quesadillas.

9. Place the quesadillas onto the lined baking trays and bake in the preheated oven for 20 minutes.

10. Leave to cool a little and cut in half to serve.

And another idea:

▶ Experiment with different types of beans (e.g. pinto, kidney, haricot) and different types of tortilla wraps (e.g. wholemeal, seeded, corn). Add a tiny sprinkle of chilli powder before folding the tortilla for those who like it spicy. Try adding finely diced red and green peppers to the filling. Substitute the black beans for a cup of cooked lean beef mince for a higher iron version.

▶ Adapt to themes by using cookie cutters to remove a shape from the top fold of the tortilla to reveal the filling inside, such as a letter, number, animal, star, etc.

▶ Try salad spinner art using paper plates and paint in the colours of the Mexican flag. The children can sprinkle on Mexican spices before the paint dries for extra texture and sensory stimulation.

▶ Set up an exploratory table for the children to look at beans and corn in pods/cobs, dried and canned.

▶ Watch beans sprout and grow on a sunny spot in clear plastic cups with damp cotton wool.

▶ Play the bean game outside or in an open space. For example, when you say 'runner bean' the children jog on the spot, if you say 'jumping bean' they jump, if you say 'baked bean' they fan their face, etc.

▶ Set up maths games using dice and pots full or large dried beans.

Prawn and vegetable Chinese spring rolls

Starter activities
Set up your role-play area with a Chinese New Year theme. Decorate the area with red and gold fabrics, hanging lanterns and dragons, floor mats, floor cushions, fans and costumes. Look at China on a globe, show the children the Chinese flag, and read a picture book on Chinese New Year. Then make prawn and vegetable Chinese spring rolls together.

Focus
Introduce different forms of vegetables and seafood with this baked version of a takeaway favourite. Filo pastry is very delicate, so a small group size works best here to enable plenty of adult support. Weigh the ingredients in advance so that the focus can be on assembling. Makes 4 spring rolls.

Skills
Weighing, measuring, mixing, scooping, careful folding, and brushing.

What you need:

Ingredients

▷ 100g finely shredded vegetables such as carrot, Chinese cabbage and beansprouts

▷ 50g cooked and peeled prawns (look for these in the chilled prepared seafood isle)

▷ 2 teaspoons reduced salt soy sauce

▷ 1/2 teaspoon minced ginger

▷ 1 teaspoon Chinese 5 Spice (check ingredients label and select one that does not contain sugar or salt)

▷ 1 teaspoon honey

▷ 2 teaspoons lemon juice or rice wine vinegar

▷ 1/2 peeled clove garlic, pressed

▷ 2 sheets of thawed filo pastry cut in half widthways to make 4 approximate squares (plus extras in case of major tears)

▷ Oil for brushing (e.g. vegetable/rapeseed)

Equipment

▷ Large mixing bowl, dessert spoons, measuring spoons and measuring cups

▷ Garlic press

▷ Weighing scales and oven gloves

▷ Pastry brushes and cups

▷ Baking sheet lined with non-stick baking paper

▷ Oven preheated to fan 180°C/350°F/Gas 4

What you do:

1. Show the children how to measure and add the soy sauce, lemon juice (or rice wine vinegar), honey, ginger, pressed garlic and Chinese 5 spice to a large bowl and mix well to make a dressing.

2. Add the vegetables and cooked prawns to the bowl and stir to thoroughly coat in the dressing.

3. For each Chinese spring roll, take a sheet of filo pastry and lay it flat on the work surface in front of each child.

4. Ask the children to lightly brush a little oil over their filo square.

5. Use a 1/4 cup measure to scoop a portion of vegetable and prawn filling. Place on the bottom edge of the filo and support the children in shaping the filling into a sausage shape, leaving 2cm side borders.

6. Fold the side borders in, and then support the children in gently rolling upwards to the top edge. Place the spring rolls onto the lined baking sheet, ensuring that they are seam-side down.

7. Ask the children to brush a little oil on the tops of the spring rolls.

8. Bake in the preheated oven for 15 minutes or until golden brown and crispy.

9. Leave to cool and cut in half before serving.

And another idea:

▶ Try different combinations of finely sliced vegetables such as spring onions, red peppers, mange tout or even cooked edamame beans.

▶ Try a dragon dance or lion dance activity with the children. Include puppets and percussion instruments to involve everyone.

▶ Visit a Chinese supermarket or takeaway/restaurant to look at ingredients see a cooking demonstration.

▶ Set up a sensory activity by filling the sand table with rice, Chinese soup bowls and spoons, chopsticks, and small world dragon figures.

▶ Try a Chinese New Year themed play dough activity by adding red and gold glitter to red play dough. Set out rectangular cutters to make red envelopes. Include black and gold pipe cleaners and play gold coins.

▶ Set up a literacy activity with a black tray and red decorative sand or dyed red salt. This can be used with fingers for mark making, tracing letters or sight words depending on the ages and stages of the children.

Vegetable Samosas

Starter activities

Introduce the Diwali festival to the children. Read Diwali themed picture books such as Diwali by Rodger Priddy. Set up a Rangoli craft activity by printing out Diwali Rangoli pattern outlines onto card. The children can then use school glue on one section at a time and sprinkle with different colour dyed rice. Then make vegetable samosas together.

Focus

Introduce different forms of vegetables and spices with a baked version of a takeaway favourite. Filo pastry is very delicate so a small group size works best here to enable plenty of adult support. Makes 4 samosas. Do a practice run beforehand to get used to the folding action.

> ### Skills
> Weighing, measuring, mixing, scooping, careful folding, and brushing.

What you need:

Ingredients

▷ 1/2 a peeled clove of garlic, pressed

▷ 1/2 teaspoon minced ginger

▷ 2 teaspoons mild curry powder

▷ 1 teaspoon oil (vegetable/rapeseed)

▷ 200g diced mixed vegetables (frozen or tinned works well here)

▷ 4 sprigs coriander

▷ 2 spring onions

▷ 2 sheets of thawed filo pastry cut in half lengthways to form 4 long rectangular sheets (plus extras in case of major tears!)

▷ Oil for brushing (e.g. vegetable/rapeseed)

Equipment

▷ Large mixing bowl, dessert spoons, measuring spoons and measuring cups

▷ Garlic press

▷ Weighing scales and oven gloves

▷ Pastry brushes and cups

▷ Clean nursery scissors, used for cooking only

▷ Baking sheet lined with non-stick baking paper

▷ Oven preheated to fan 180°C/350°F/Gas 4

What you do:

1. Show the children how to use the measuring spoons to measure and add the pressed garlic, minced ginger, curry powder, and oil to a large bowl and mix well to make a dressing.

2. Add the mixed vegetables to the bowl, and support the children in using the scissors to snip in the spring onions. Then tear in the coriander leaves and snip in their stalks. Stir all the ingredients in the bowl to thoroughly coat in the dressing.

3. For each samosa, lay one sheet of filo pastry horizontally across the work surface in front of each child. Ask the children to very lightly brush a little oil across their filo sheet.

4. Use a 1/4 cup measure to scoop a portion of the filling and place on the bottom left corner of the filo.

5. Work with each child to carefully fold the top left corner down to cover the filling and form a triangle. Continue to fold the triangular parcel towards the right, maintaining the triangular shape, until you reach the end of the pastry sheet.

6. Place the samosa onto the lined baking sheet, ensuring that the loose edge of filo is tucked underneath the parcel. Then, ask the children to brush the tops of each samosa with a little oil.

7. Bake in the preheated oven for 15 minutes or until golden brown and crispy. Leave to cool and cut in half before serving.

And another idea:

► You can substitute the garlic, ginger, curry powder and oil in the filling with a tablespoon of mild-medium Indian curry paste.

► Try making decorative Diyas/Divas by shaping a tealight holder out of dyed salt dough, and adding glitter, sequins and beads before drying. Do send a note home to parents that it is for decorative use only.

► Set up a firework printing art activity with black paper. Make stamps with the children by twisting a bunch of pipe cleaners and fanning out one end. The children can use these with dishes of bright paint as stamps to print their fireworks.

► Set up a play dough burfi activity by mixing ground cardamom and desiccated coconut into play dough. Set out bright, colourful paper plates, rolling pins and diamond and triangle shaped cookie cutters.

► Listen to traditional Diwali stick dance music and encourage the children to dance along holding decorated cardboard tube 'sticks'.

► Visit any Diwali festival displays happening in your local community.

Roasted vegetable curry

Starter activities

Transform your role-play area into an Indian take-away kitchen with a cardboard box oven, pans, cooking utensils, a large foil circular disposable tray to use as a chapatti griddle, a spice box, pulse containers, vegetables models, takeaway tubs, paper bags, aprons, a telephone and notepad for orders, a counter and a cash register. Talk with the children about any Indian foods that they like to eat and use specific language to describe tastes and textures. Then come together to make roasted vegetable curry.

Focus

This is a great introduction for the children in making their own main course. Depending on the ages and stages of the children, and the availability of adult support, you may choose to chop the vegetables in advance and involve the children in snapping the stalks off of the green beans or snipping the spring onions.

Skills

Chopping (depending on ages, stages and support availability), snipping, measuring, and mixing.

What you need:

Ingredients

- ▷ 120g sweet potato, peeled and chopped into 1-2cm dice
- ▷ 150g courgette, chopped into 1-2cm dice
- ▷ 150g cherry tomatoes, quartered
- ▷ 120g cauliflower, chopped into very small florets
- ▷ 110g green beans, stalks removed
- ▷ 3 spring onions
- ▷ 130g drained canned chickpeas
- ▷ 2 tablespoons mild-medium Indian curry paste
- ▷ 3 tablespoons natural yoghurt
- ▷ Cooked rice, chapatti, roti or naan to serve

Equipment

- ▷ Vegetable knife and chopping board
- ▷ Clean nursery scissors, reserved for kitchen use only
- ▷ Measuring spoons, mixing spoons and a non-stick slotted spatula
- ▷ Weighing scales, large mixing bowl and large serving bowl
- ▷ Non-stick rimmed baking tray and oven gloves
- ▷ Oven preheated to fan 200°C/425°F/Gas 7

What you do:

1. Ask the children to add the prepared sweet potato, courgette, cauliflower, cherry tomatoes and chickpeas to a large mixing bowl.

2. Support the children in safely snipping in the green beans and spring onions.

3. Show the children how to use the measuring spoons to measure and add the curry paste. Then they can take turns to mix well until all the vegetables are coated.

4. Empty the mixing bowl onto the rimmed baking sheet and ask the children to help spread the vegetables out evenly.

5. Roast in the preheated oven for 25 minutes or until the vegetables are tender and the cauliflower is just beginning to char at the edges.

6. Place the roasted curry vegetables into a large serving bowl. Add the yoghurt and mix well.

7. Serve with rice, chapatti, roti or naan.

And another idea:

▶ Try other vegetables that are easily prepared, such as sugar snap peas or baby sweetcorn that the children can snap into bite-sized chunks. Try tearing in some coriander leaves before serving.

▶ Have a spice smelling session (not with chilli). Then, use the spices for a sensory art session by adding them to watered-down glue to paint spicy pictures with.

▶ Try a spice themed literacy activity. Write each child's name large on separate pieces of card. The children can trace their name with a small squeezy bottle of glue. Provide a spice box with a selection of spices in egg cups for the children to sprinkle over their names. This could also be used for letters, sight words or numbers.

▶ Set up a chai tea water play activity in the water table with chai tea infused water, aluminium kettle/teapots, small clay pot cups and ladles. The children can add the milk, and drop in star anise to float in the mixture. You could add small plastic spoons marked with numbers to add some number naming fun.

▶ Visit a local Indian supermarket or arrange a tour of an Indian restaurant/ takeaway kitchen.

Fun fruity fondue

Starter activities

Focus on a fruit theme with a fruit market stall role-play activity. Set up a stall with a counter, canopy, sign, baskets and large bowls filled with fruit models, shopping baskets, paper bags, balance scales, aprons, cash register, play money and shopping lists with words and pictures. Read 'Oliver's Fruit Salad' by Vivian French and then come together to make fun fruity fondue.

Focus

Make a fruit dessert to share and enjoy. This tasty treat offers an opportunity to explore a variety of fruits and taste them in a novel way. This can be linked back to the Eatwell Plate and 5-a-day.

Skills

Identifying fruits, naming their colours and counting them. Preparation methods including washing, peeling, chopping, mashing, and mixing.

What you need:

Ingredients

▷ 2 bananas

▷ 2 tangerines

▷ 100g of green seedless grapes

▷ 100g of red seedless grapes

▷ 120g of ripe strawberries, stalks removed

▷ 200g of Greek yoghurt (standard or reduced fat)

▷ 1 tablespoon of runny honey

Equipment

▷ Table knives and chopping boards

▷ Bowl of water and clean cloth

▷ Large zip lock bags

▷ Serving platter and soup bowl

▷ Forks or skewers

▷ Fun optional extra: crinkle cutter

What you do:

1. Look at the selection of ingredients. Note the colours, shapes, and number of each fruit. How do they feel to hold (weight, texture)?

2. Prepare the bananas. The children can practice peeling the skin. You may need to start this off for them. They can then place the peeled bananas onto a chopping board and either break them apart into chunks, or cut into chunks with a table knife. If you have a crinkle cutter, this can be a fun way to introduce children to chopping. To practice other fine motor skills, you could slice the banana with the skin on (using a paring knife) and then let the children practice pulling the strips of peel from each slice. Add the chunks of banana to the platter.

3. Peel the tangerines. You can start it off and show the children how to use their fingers to pull off pieces of the skin. Alternatively you can break the tangerine in half and the children can pull out the segments and separate them. Show them how to hold the segments up to the light to check for pips. Add the tangerine segments to the platter.

4. Plunge the grapes into the bowl of water and ask the children to gently wash. Pat them dry with a clean cloth. The children can pluck the grapes from the stalks. Note the different colours of grapes. Ask: 'Is the taste different too?' Add the grapes to the platter.

5. Make the strawberry yoghurt fondue dip. Put the strawberries into the zip lock bag. Press most of the air out and close the zip. Let the children pass the bag around the table so that everyone can take a turn squashing the strawberries with the palm of their hands by pressing the bag onto the table. Discuss how this feels and how the appearance of the strawberries changes. Tip the squashed strawberries into the soup bowl with the Greek yoghurt and mix to combine. Add a little honey to taste, depending on the sweetness of the strawberries.

6. Give each child a skewer or fork and let the fondue fun begin as they spear the fruit pieces and dip into the strawberry yoghurt. If double-dipping is a concern, adapt the presentation with individual fondues.

And another idea:

▶ Try themed fruit fondue sessions such as tropical fruits, seasonal fruits, or colour themes, such as 'eat a rainbow'.

▶ Pick some garden mint, snip into small pieces in a mug using clean nursery scissors. Add to the yoghurt dip for a refreshing twist.

▶ Any leftover peel, skin or pips could be used for a composting activity.

▶ Read picture books that include fruit such as 'The Very Hungry Caterpillar' by Eric Carle and 'Handa's Surprise' by Eileen Browne.

▶ Try a colour sorting activity using tongs and a mini model fruit set.

▶ Introduce some dramatic play by getting the children to imagine that they are a tiny fruit seed, curled up in a ball in the soil. Then they are watered and the sun shines. Slowly they begin to sprout, push out leaves, grow bigger and bigger into a plant. The bees visit them and they flower and fruit.

▶ Grow fruits in your outdoor space or in containers. Strawberry or miniature blueberry bushes work well and are easy to maintain.

▶ Visit a local fruit market stall, community orchard or 'pick your own' fruit farm.

▶ Label a muffin tin with numbers 1-12 and provide a bunch of grapes for children to pull off and sort into the muffin cups.

Peach beach cup

Starter activities

Transform your area into a beach! Set up a parasol and lay out beach towels, sun hats, sunglasses, beach balls, empty sunscreen bottles and body boards. Create a rock pool in a paddling pool by adding rocks, seaweed, crabs, shells, buckets and nets. Talk about the importance of staying safe in the sun. Then make a peach beach cup together.

Focus

A fun twist on a traditional cheesecake recipe that demonstrates how fresh and tinned fruit can count towards your 5-a-day.

Skills

Measuring, scooping, spooning, and mixing.

What you need:

Ingredients

▷ 250g soft cheese (standard or reduced fat)

▷ 1/2 teaspoon vanilla extract

▷ 1 1/2 x 410g tins of peach halves in juice (not syrup), drained

▷ 250g diced strawberries, washed

▷ 6 oat biscuits or digestive biscuits

▷ Natural blue food colouring (this is now available in most supermarkets and is often made with spirulina extract)

Equipment

▷ Small mixing bowls

▷ Measuring spoons and dessert spoons

▷ Tin opener

▷ Hand blender and suitable high sided beaker

▷ Pestle and mortar

▷ Cocktail parasols

▷ Small plastic cups (transparent, so that children can see the layers)

What you do:

1. Ask the children to empty the soft cheese into a small mixing bowl.

2. Show them how to use the measuring spoons to add the vanilla to the soft cheese.

3. Add 3 drops of natural blue food colouring and ask the children to take turns to mix well until smooth.

4. The children can watch you blend the drained peaches until you have a smooth puree. This is a good opportunity to discuss safety around sharp equipment.

5. Ask the children to add 8 tablespoons of peach puree to the blue soft cheese. You can all count the spoons together. Mix well until smooth. You may wish to add a drop more natural blue food colouring if the colour is a little murky.

6. Give each child a small clear plastic cup. Ask them to add 2 dessert spoons of the blue soft cheese mixture and then jiggle their cup until the layer flattens.

7. Next, ask the children to add 2 dessert spoons of peach puree to their cup.

8. Ask them to add 1-2 dessert spoons diced strawberries for the next layer.
9. Place the biscuits into a pestle and mortar and ask the children to crush them until it resembles sand. They can then use a dessert spoon to scoop a layer of biscuit 'sand' for the top layer in their cup.
10. Finally, decorate by adding a cocktail parasol to each cup!

And another idea:

▶ Try adding a little lemon zest to the soft cheese for extra tang.

▶ Read 'Each Peach Pear Plum' by Janet and Allan Ahlberg or 'Sharing a Shell' by Julia Donaldson.

▶ Set up a seashell treasure hunt in your outdoor space, with beach buckets for collection and counting.

▶ Have a fun physical activity session with beach balls and a parachute.

▶ Add water to the sand in your sandpit so the children can try some sandcastle construction play.

Jelly ponds

Starter activities

Fill your water table with water coloured green, and add white or black water beads for a frogspawn effect. Cut lily pads out of green craft foam sheets and add small-world pond-life, plastic fish tank plants, and pebbles. Talk about the lifecycle of a frog and look at a 'pond life' pictorial reference book. Then make jelly ponds.

Focus

Make your own no added sugar fruit juice jelly. Makes 6 small jelly pots.

Skills

Mixing, scooping, pouring – and waiting!

What you need:

Ingredients

▷ 4 teaspoons of unsweetened powdered gelatine. Note: gelatine contains animal products. Beware of any special, ethnic, or religious diets. If you use a vegetarian gelatine substitute here, adapt the recipe and method according to the manufacturer's instructions.

▷ 100ml hot water

▷ 450ml apple juice (100% fruit juice, unsweetened, not from concentrate)

▷ 240g blueberries

Equipment

▷ Large measuring jug

▷ Forks and dessert spoons

▷ 6 small transparent cups

▷ Small tray or large plate

What you do:

1. Ask the children to use dessert spoons to divide the blueberries evenly between the 6 transparent cups.

2. Add the powdered gelatine to the jug of hand hot water. Let the children take turns mixing with a fork until the gelatine has completely dissolved.

3. Add the apple juice and take turns mixing again.

4. Assist the children in pouring the jelly mixture evenly into the 6 cups. Place the cups onto a small tray or large plate.

5. Next comes the waiting bit! Refrigerate for 3 hours, or until set.

And another idea:

▶ Pour the fruit and jelly mixture into lolly moulds and freeze for a hot weather treat with a novel texture.

▶ Try other fruit juices and other soft fruits such as raspberries, halved grapes, or pineapple chunks.

▶ Have fun making your own fruit juice for this recipe with a lever-arm juicer and a pile of oranges.

▶ Visit a nature reserve or go pond dipping (using safe supervision) to look for real frogspawn.

▶ Sing 'Five Little Speckled Frogs' using a play mirror and frog beanbags to act out the story.

▶ Set up a lily pad jumping game with large green lily pads cut out of thin rubber sheets. Write numbers, letters or sight words on top of each lily pad for a physical numeracy or literacy play session.

▶ Read 'In the Pond' by Anna Milbourne and 'The Jelly That Wouldn't Wobble' by Angela Mitchell.

Further reading and resources

Advisory Panel on Food and Nutrition in Early Years (2011) Laying the Table: Recommendations for National Food and Nutrition Guidance for Early Years settings in England [Online] Available at www.childrensfoodtrust.org.uk/apfney

Allergy UK www.allergyuk.org

British Dietetic Association Food Fact Sheets www.bda.uk.com/foodfacts/home

British Nutrition Foundation www.nutrition.org.uk

Caroline Walker Trust www.cwt.org.uk/publications/

Change4Life for Early Years Providers www.nhs.uk/Change4Life/Pages/nurseries-childrens-centres-supporters.aspx

Children's Food Trust www.childrensfoodtrust.org.uk/pre-school

Children's Food Trust early years webpage www.childrensfoodtrust.org.uk/eatbetterstartbetter

Children's Food Trust (2008) British Food Chart www.childrensfoodtrust.org.uk/resources/seasonalitychart

Department for Education (2014) 'Statutory Framework for the Early Years Foundation Stage: Setting the standards for learning, development and care for children from birth to five' www.gov.uk/government/uploads/system/uploads/attachment_data/file/335504/EYFS_framework_from_1_September_2014__with_clarification_note.pdf

Food a Fact of Life www.foodafactoflife.org.uk

Growing Schools: Early Years Resource Bank www.growingschools.org.uk/resources/library?keystage=5 Healthy Start www.healthystart.nhs.uk/

Infant and Toddler Forum www.littlepeoplesplates.co.uk

Let's Get Cooking www.letsgetcooking.org.uk

Marine Stewardship Council www.msc.org

National Child Measurement Programme - England 2013-2014 www.hscic.gov.uk/catalogue/PUB16070/nati-chil-meas-prog-eng-2013-2014-rep.pdf

NHS Choices: Food Allergy www.nhs.uk/conditions/food-allergy/pages/intro1.aspx

NHS Choices Food labels www.nhs.uk/Livewell/Goodfood/Pages/food-labelling.aspx

NHS Choices: The Eatwell Plate www.nhs.uk/Livewell/Goodfood/Pages/eatwell-plate.aspx

NHS Choices: Vitamins for Children www.nhs.uk/conditions/pregnancy-and-baby/pages/vitamins-for-children.aspx#close

Nursery Milk Scheme www.nurserymilk.co.uk/index.html

Royal Horticultural Society www.rhs.org.uk/Children

Safer food, better business, Food Standards Agency www.food.gov.uk/foodindustry/regulation/hygleg/hyglegresources/sfbb/

The Early Years Foundation Stage (Welfare Requirements) Regulations 2012 (S.I. 2012/938). Available at: www.legislation.gov.uk/uksi/2012/938/made

The Eatwell Plate: how to use it in promotional material www.gov.uk/government/publications/the-eatwell-plate-how-to-use-it-in-promotional-material

The Vegan Society www.vegansociety.com

The Vegetarian Society www.vegsoc.org